DAVID
AND
GOLIATH

For Ken Doroshow, a Spoke
among spokes—E. M.

To Linda and our walks
along the river with Marge
chasing sticks in the
water. Thanks for
your support and
understanding. —D. F.

Rabbit Ears Books is an imprint of Rabbit Ears Productions, Inc.
Published by Simon & Schuster, Inc.
1230 Avenue of the Americas
New York, New York 10020

Copyright © 1996 Rabbit Ears Productions, Inc.,
Rowayton, Connecticut.

Manufactured in the United States of America.
10 9 8 7 6 5 4 3 2 1

Library of Congress Cataloging-in-Publication Data

Metaxas, Eric.
David and Goliath / written by Eric Metaxas ; illustrated by Douglas Fraser.
p. cm.
Summary: Retells the Bible story of the shepherd boy who saved his people
by killing a giant.
ISBN 0-689-80604-3
1. David, King of Israel—Juvenile literature. 2. Goliath (Biblical giant)—
Juvenile literature. 3. Bible stories, English—O.T. [1. David, King of Israel.
2. Goliath (Biblical giant) 3. Bible stories—O.T.] I. Fraser, Douglas, 1961– ill.
II. Title
BS580.D3M38 1996
222'.4309505—dc20
92-36282
CIP
AC

DAVID
AND
GOLIATH

Written by
ERIC METAXAS
Illustrated by
DOUGLAS FRASER

RABBIT EARS BOOKS

From the days of Abraham, Isaac, and Jacob to the days of Moses, who led them out of Egypt and slavery, to the days of Joshua, who took them into the Promised Land, all the way to the days of Samuel, who was their judge and priest, the people of Israel had never had a king. Each of the nations that surrounded them had a king, but Israel remained alone in being led not by any man, but by God himself.

Now, the people of ancient Israel were not very different from other people at other times: They longed to have what they did not. And so they went to Samuel, whom God had appointed judge and priest over them, demanding: "Give us a king, like the other nations!"

Samuel knew that in wishing for a king the Israelites were really rejecting God, and he grieved over it. He tried to change their minds, but they would not listen and so, not knowing what to do, Samuel prayed to the Lord for guidance.

Then the Lord spoke to Samuel: "If they do not want my will to be done, I shall let their will be done. Arise, Samuel! Give them their king of flesh and blood."

And so Samuel rose up and anointed Saul to be king over the Israelites.

Now because his military successes were great in number, the people of Israel were pleased to have him as their king. But in many of the things that Saul did, he neglected the Lord. Samuel saw all of this, and just as he had mourned when God's people had asked for a king, he now mourned for the king who they had chosen. And as Saul's unfaithfulness toward God continued, Samuel's grief over it increased.

Then one day the Lord came to Samuel. "How long will you mourn for Saul?" the Lord said. "Arise, Samuel, and go to Bethlehem. Take a horn of oil and find there a man named Jesse, for I have selected one of his sons to be the new king over my people. He will not be like Saul, but will be my obedient servant."

"But Lord," Samuel said, "if Saul discovers that I am anointing a new king, he will seek to kill me."

"Do not fear, Samuel," the Lord said. "Say to the people of Bethlehem that you have come to make a sacrifice. When you are sanctifying the people of Bethlehem in preparation for the sacrifice I will show you which one of Jesse's sons to anoint."

And so Samuel took a heifer for the sacrifice and traveled to Bethlehem, amazed at the faithfulness of the Lord.

When the elders of Bethlehem saw the old prophet of God approaching, they were greatly disturbed, for Samuel's appearance usually meant that God was going to proclaim a judgment upon them for their sins. But Samuel assured them that all was well and he prepared them to partake in the sacrifice. Then he called Jesse and his sons to come to the sacrifice, and he sanctified Jesse and then turned to Jesse's sons, wondering which one of them the Lord would choose to be Israel's next king.

When Samuel saw Jesse's firstborn, Eliab, he thought, surely this is the one whom the Lord has chosen, for Eliab was tall and handsome in his appearance. But the Lord said that Eliab was not the one.

"Do not look at his face or stature," the Lord said to Samuel, "for this is not my chosen. I do not see the way men see. Men look at the outward appearance, but I, the Lord your God, look into a man's heart."

And so the first of Jesse's sons passed in front of Samuel and then the second and then the third on down to the seventh and the Lord chose none of them.

Samuel was puzzled. "Are all your sons here?" he asked.

"There remains yet another named David," Jesse replied, "who is the youngest of all my sons. He is out in the fields feeding my flocks."

"Then send for him," Samuel said, "for we will not sit down to eat until he has arrived."

Now David was often found in the wilderness, tending his father's sheep. Even though there was danger when a wild animal came to attack the flock or when one of the sheep became lost, David rejoiced at the time he could spend there. As he wandered about with his flocks he would spend countless hours playing his lyre and his spirit would soar above the clouds as he sang praises to God.

"The Lord is my shepherd," he sang. "I shall not want. He maketh me to lie down in green pastures and leadeth me beside the still waters. He restoreth my soul. He leadeth me in the paths of righteousness for his name's sake. Yea, though I walk through the valley of the shadow of death, I will fear no evil, for thou art with me; thy rod and thy staff they comfort me."

David acknowledged God in all his ways, and so, when his brother came to fetch him on behalf of God's prophet, Samuel, David did not tarry but came quickly.

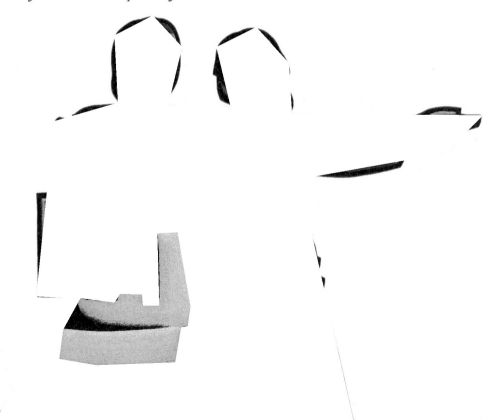

After a time Samuel looked and saw something like a rising sun floating on the horizon in the distance across the fields of Bethlehem, and he rubbed his old eyes, unable to make it out. But when it came nearer he saw that it was a simple redheaded lad dressed in shepherd's clothing and carrying a shepherd's staff.

At that moment the Lord spoke to Samuel's heart. "Arise, Samuel, and anoint this one for he is my chosen who will be king over my beloved people, Israel."

Then Samuel arose, took the horn of oil and stepping forward he anointed David in the midst of his brothers. The oil ran over his head and over his body and the spirit of the Lord poured out of the heavens and came down upon David in great power and remained with him from that day forward.

Now, because of Saul's great disobedience, the spirit of God had left him and Saul became filled with great fear and depression. His servants saw that their king was not himself, and they feared for themselves and for all of Israel. Then one of the servants thought of a solution. "Let one of us go and search for someone who is skilled in playing the lyre," he said to Saul. "Whenever you are tormented he will play upon the lyre and you will be well again."

Then another of the servants spoke: "I know of one who lives in Bethlehem," he said. "He is a shepherd boy, the son of Jesse, and he plays the lyre while he is out in the fields watching his flocks. And the spirit of the Lord is with him."

Now Saul had no idea that Samuel had anointed this David to be king over Israel, and he wanted to do anything to be rid of the dark moods that had been tormenting him, so he sent messengers to Bethlehem to speak with Jesse.

Jesse was pleased that the king desired his son's presence and he agreed to let him go, sending with him a donkey laden with bread and a skin of wine and a kid from his flocks.

When David came into Saul's presence, Saul was greatly taken with the young man. His songs of praise to God touched Saul's heart deeply and the dark moods that afflicted him seemed to disappear when David played. And so Saul made David his own personal armor bearer and whenever Saul was tormented he would send for David and David would play his lyre, and immediately Saul's black mood would depart.

Now during all the years that Saul was king, the Israelites were in a continuous war against the Philistines, who were a neighboring tribe that worshipped many gods. It was sometimes the custom in those days to decide battles by having the champion of one side fight that of the enemy.

But there arose out of the ranks of the Philistines a champion from Gath named Goliath. Goliath was truly a giant of a man, for he stood nearly nine feet tall, and when the Israelites saw him they trembled. He was unlike anything anyone had ever imagined. On his head he wore a brass helmet and on his huge body a coat of mail that weighed nearly two hundred pounds. His legs were covered with brass greaves and he carried a giant spear tipped with an iron spearhead that weighed twenty-five pounds.

He boldly challenged the Israelites to send a man to fight with him, taunting them and boasting and strutting on the battlefield.

"Why are you standing there?" he shouted mockingly. "Can it be that there is no man among the Israelites willing to come against me in battle?"

There were many brave warriors among Saul's army, but none so brave that he dared come against this Philistine monster. They trembled at his sight and murmured amongst themselves. "Who is this Goliath?" they said. "And who is able to make war with him?"

Goliath struck fear even in the heart of Saul, who was a huge man and a brave warrior himself. Saul wrung his hands in fear, for it appeared that unless something were done, the Philistines would at last have total victory over the Israelites.

For forty days the Philistine giant challenged them, daring the Israelites to fight, and for forty days the Israelites shook with fear, unable to find a single challenger from among their ranks.

Now it so happened that David had been traveling back and forth between Shiloh and Bethlehem in order to take care of his father's sheep. Jesse was anxious to discover the fate of his three sons who were in Saul's army, and so he gave David some food and sent him to Shiloh to find out how his brothers were faring.

When David arrived the Philistine Goliath from Gath was again strutting on the plain of battle, daring the Israelites to send a man to do battle with him. But when David saw the Israelites trembling at the sight of Goliath, he grew angry.

"Who is this Philistine that dares defy the armies of the living God?" he asked.

When Eliab saw that his youngest brother was stirring up trouble he became displeased. "What are you doing here?" he said. "You have no business among soldiers! Who is taking care of your sheep in Bethlehem?"

But David persisted. "This is not right!" he said. "Who is that Philistine that he dare defy the armies of the Lord God? God will not allow it! He will give that overgrown heathen into our hands!"

The soldiers were taken aback at David's courage, but he became increasingly frustrated at their fearfulness. "God is faithful to his people!" he said. "Surely he will deliver this puffed-up blasphemer into our hands!"

But none of the soldiers was quite as convinced of this as David was. One of them, hearing David's words, reported them to King Saul, who sent for David.

I know you are a servant of the Lord," Saul said, "and that you are brave and zealous for God and have great faith, but this Goliath is unlike anything anyone has ever seen."

David was undaunted, though. "When Moses stood up against Pharaoh the Lord was with him!" he said. "And when Joshua stormed Jericho it was not by his might, but by the Lord's. Therefore, if no one else will go, I, David, your servant, will go and fight this Philistine."

"But you are still a youth, David," Saul said, "and this Philistine is an experienced soldier. You don't stand a chance against him!"

T hen David told the king a story. "When I have been out in the wilderness keeping my father's sheep, lions have come, and bears, and they have stolen away my lambs. But each time I have left my father's flocks to go after the one that was lost, and each time with nothing more than my shepherd's club and staff, I have fought and regained what was stolen. Even when the great beasts have turned to come against me, I have killed them. But it is not me who does it, but the Lord. And the same Lord who delivered me and my sheep from the paws of the lions and bears in the wilderness will deliver me out of the hands of this Philistine."

"Then go," said Saul, "and the Lord be with you."

But before he went, Saul gave David his armor, putting on his head a helmet of brass and arming him with a coat of mail. He gave him also a sword. "Now you are outfitted as Goliath is!" Saul said.

But David had never worn soldier's armor before. "I cannot go with these things," he said. "I am not used to them." With that he took them off and left Saul's chamber wearing only his shepherd's clothing.

Then David stopped by a brook and selected five smooth stones, which he put into his shepherd's bag. And as he made his way toward the battlefield, he sang out in joy:

"The Lord is my light and my salvation;
whom shall I fear?
The Lord is the strength of my life;
of whom shall I be afraid?"

Word that David would challenge Goliath had traveled very quickly throughout the entire Israelite army, and when David finally strode through the ranks toward the battlefield every eye was upon him. The soldiers marveled at him, wondering what sort of person he was: for he looked nothing like a warrior, and he carried neither sword nor spear nor shield, and he wore no helmet nor any armor at all.

David heard them talking and he could hear Goliath roaring his threats and taunts.

"Does not a single Israelite have any courage? Where is your God that you cower so?"

But David's heart was not anxious, and as he approached the battlefield he sang as sweetly as though he were under a tree with his lyre, watching his father's flocks.

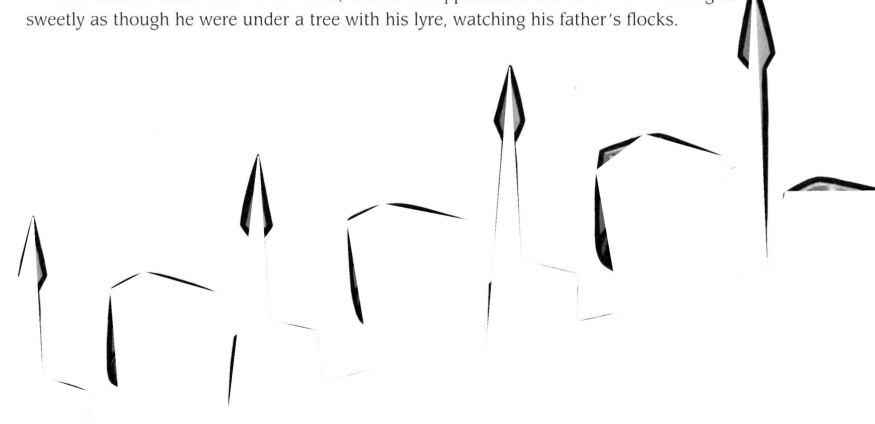

When at last he strode onto the field of battle to confront Goliath, the Philistine soldiers saw him and laughed. But Goliath did not laugh. He could not believe what his eyes saw and he stared in amazement at this curious youth who wore no armor and carried only a shepherd's staff.

"Perhaps you think I am a dog that you should come to fight me with a stick!" he roared. "In the name of my gods I curse you and your people and I curse the name of the god you serve! Step forward now that I might give your flesh to the birds of the air and the beasts of the field!"

Hearing these words David did not move forward or backward. He only stood where he was. "You come to me with a sword and a shield and a spear," he shouted in reply, "but I come to you in the name of the Holy One of Israel, the Most High God of Heaven and Earth, whom you have cursed! And it is he, not I, who will deliver you into my hand this day, so that everyone will know that there is one god in Israel."

Goliath burned on hearing these words, but David continued. "The Lord does not need a sword as you do, or a spear as you do, or a shield as you do, because the battle belongs to him and him alone!"

Goliath could hear no more of this. He came across the field toward David and the air was rent with the clanking sound of his heavy armor. But David was not frightened, and the moment that he saw the huge Philistine approaching him, he started running toward him as fast as he could. Goliath was stunned to see this for he could not comprehend the young Israelite's boldness. Before Goliath knew what was happening, David plucked one of the stones out of his bag, put it in the pocket of his sling and, with an incredible power that was not his own, he whirled it over his head. Then he let it go, and with the surging crack of a lightning bolt, it struck Goliath's forehead, a dead bull's-eye.

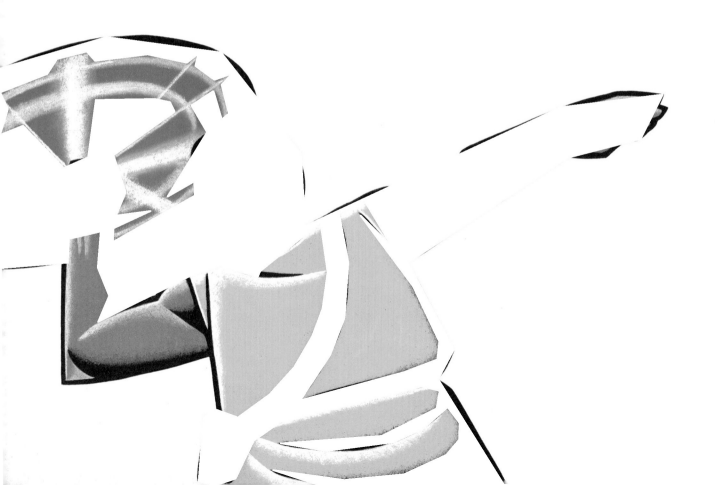

There was an instant of perfect silence as ten thousand men held their breath. Every Philistine and every Israelite saw that the smooth stone had hit its mark. No one moved.

Then, as though time stood still, the giant's legs buckled and he fell and fell and fell, crashing at long last into the dusty plain in an endless and vain jangling of useless armor that washed out over the stunned ranks in ever-widening waves, on and on and on, until it had spent itself and was again eclipsed by the powerful silence of the valley. Thus David defeated the giant Philistine, Goliath from Gath.

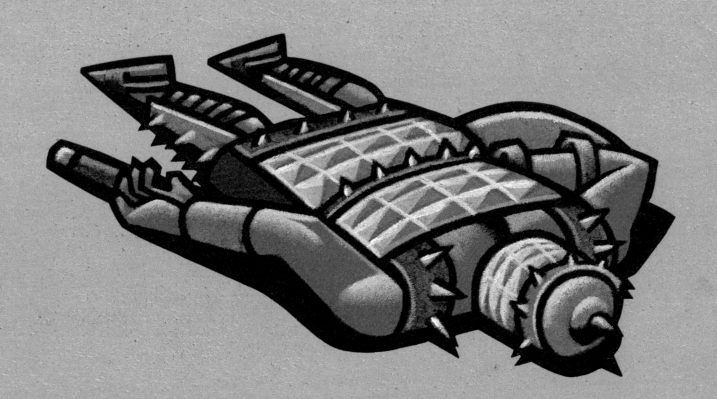

David continued to serve the Lord with all his heart, and in God's time, just as it had been ordained so many years before on the day that Samuel anointed him, David became a great king over the nation of Israel. He brought them great victories and reigned over them for many years. And in all his ways, great and small, he acknowledged the Lord his God, the Holy One of Israel.